Maths for the brighter child

AGE 3–5

D1789281

Sue Barraclough
Educational consultant: Margaret Deehan
Illustrated by Louise Comfort

This workbook provides challenging activities for the child who has made a good start in maths and is already familiar with numbers 1 to 20 and can tackle simple sums. The exercises will help your child make further progress in maths by developing the following skills and concepts:

- read and write number shapes and names up to 20
- learn number sequence
- recognise maths symbols (+ − x ÷ =)
- notice number patterns and sequences

How to help your child

- Keep sessions short (about 20 minutes) and regular.
- The exercises are intended to be enjoyable as well as educational. It is important that children discover that maths can be fun, so always stop if they are not relaxed or have lost concentration.
- Go through each page to make sure children understand what they have to do.
- Build confidence. Be positive and offer plenty of praise and encouragement. Many parents feel under-confident about maths and it is easy for this feeling to pass on to a child.
- Have at least four different coloured felt-tip pens or soft pencils to use to do the exercises. Children can see clearly what they have done and picking up and putting down the different pens is good practice in itself.
- Use practical opportunities as often as possible to explore numbers and solve simple problems.
- Counting and writing numbers are only part of what children need to learn. It is important that they understand what numbers mean and how they are used so that they can develop their own methods for working things out.

Hodder
Children's
Books

The only home learning programme supported by the NCPTA

Number names

Write each number name as a figure in the box.

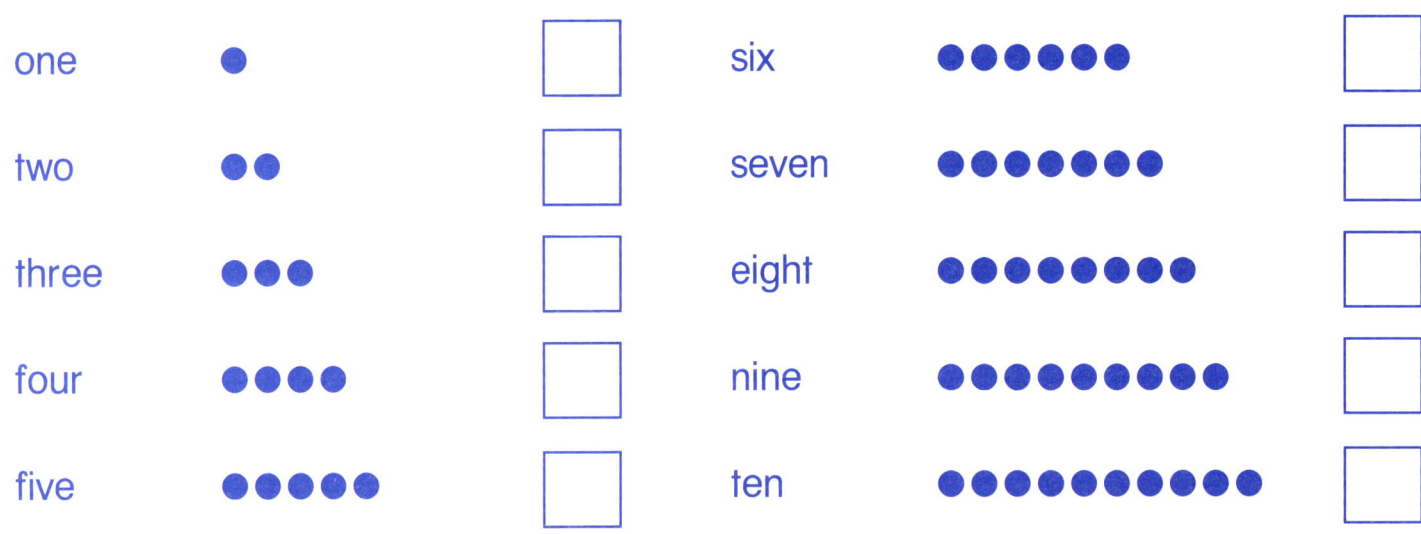

Draw the right number of dots to complete each jigsaw.

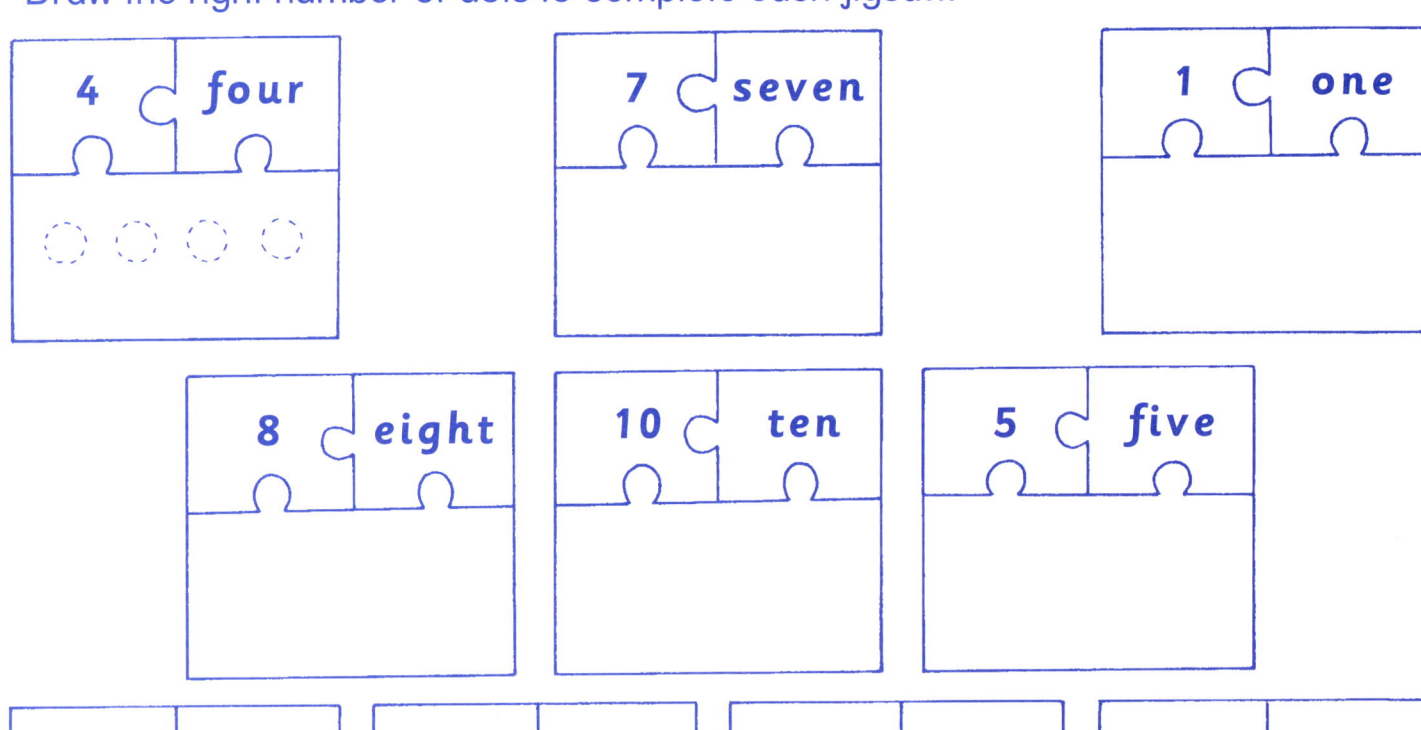

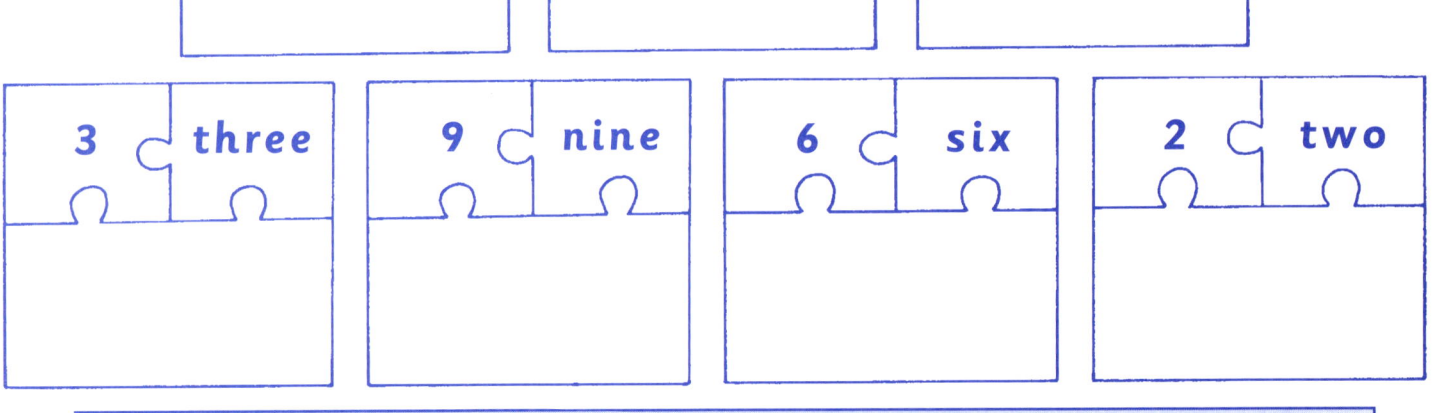

eleven	••••• ••••••	☐	sixteen	•••••••••• ••••••	☐
twelve	••••• •••••••	☐	seventeen	•••••••••• •••••••	☐
thirteen	••••• ••••••••	☐	eighteen	•••••••••• ••••••••	☐
fourteen	••••••• •••••••	☐	nineteen	•••••••••• •••••••••	☐
fifteen	••••••• ••••••••	☐	twenty	•••••••••• ••••••••••	☐

There are 10 bits of coal in each truck. Draw more bits of coal to make the total match the number on the engine.

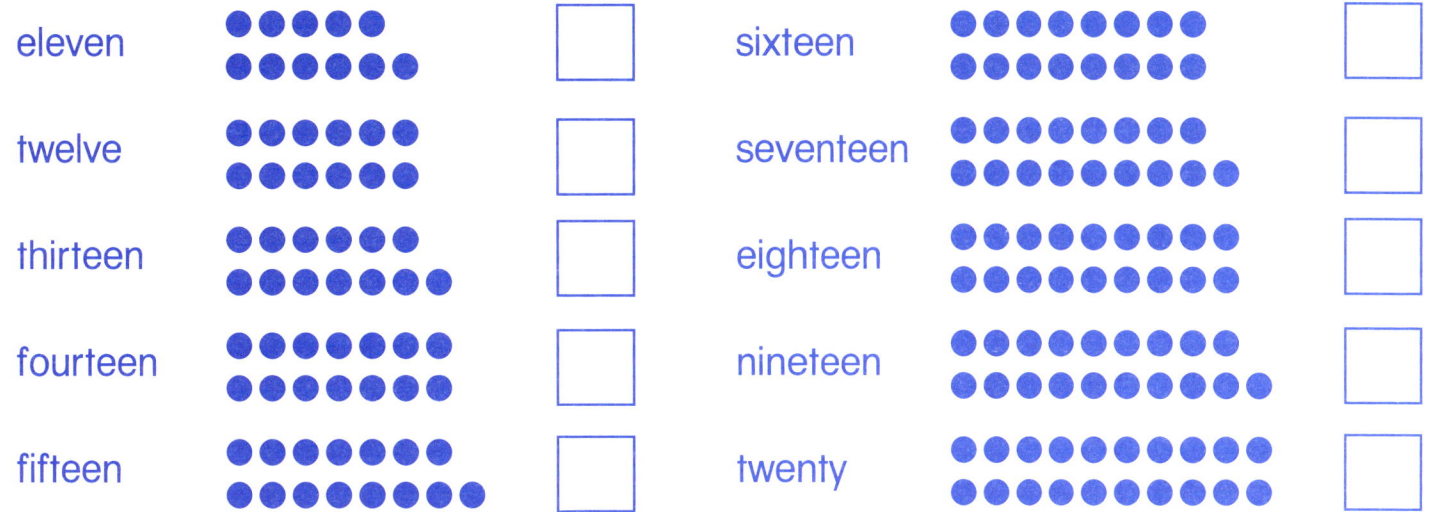

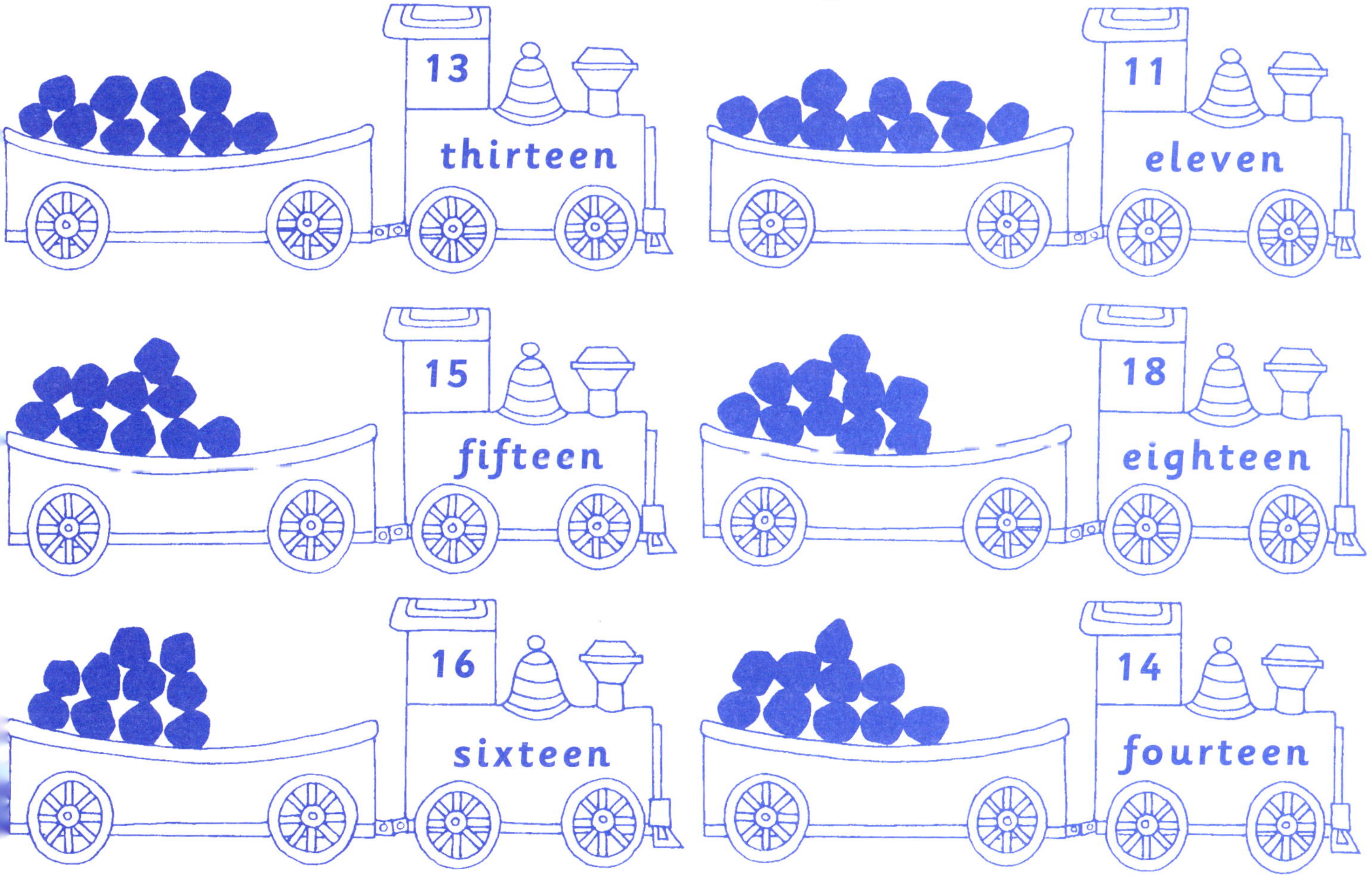

13 thirteen

11 eleven

15 fifteen

18 eighteen

16 sixteen

14 fourteen

Adding up

Write the answer to each sum in the box.

3 apples.

Add 1 more.

How many
all together?

4 carrots.

Add 2 more.

How many
all together?

These two sums can also be written like this:

3 + 1 = 4   **4 + 2 = 6**

+ means **plus** or **add**   **=** means **equals** or **all together**

You need to add up to find the answer to each of these sums.
Write the numbers and the answer in the boxes.

You buy 2 strawberry
yoghurts and
2 banana yoghurts.
How many yoghurts
do you buy all together?

 **+** **=**

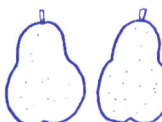

You eat 1 apple and 2 pears.
How many pieces of fruit
do you eat all together?

 **+**  **=**

Your child may find the language and symbols of 'school' maths confusing. Children can often solve
problems in their heads but the same problem written as a sum makes no sense. This simple
introduction should help link the informal maths done at home and more formal school maths.

You have 3 black pencils
and 3 stripy pencils.
How many pencils do you
have all together?

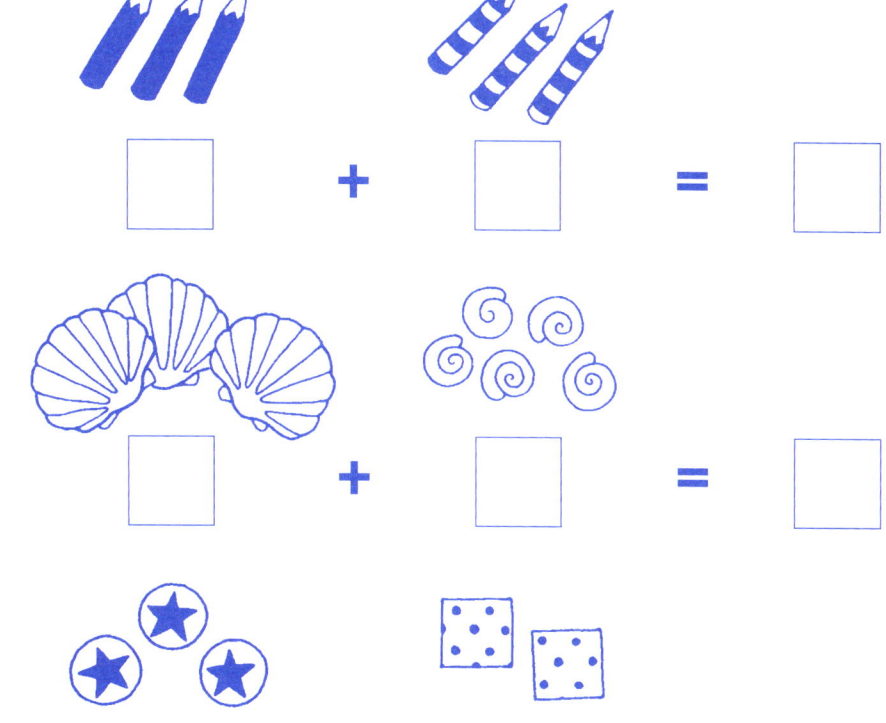

□ + □ = □

You find 3 big shells
and 5 small shells.
How many shells
do you find all together?

□ + □ = □

You have 3 round beads
and 2 square beads.
How many beads
do you have all together?

□ + □ = □

Write the answers to these adding up sums after
the = sign. Use the number beads to help you.

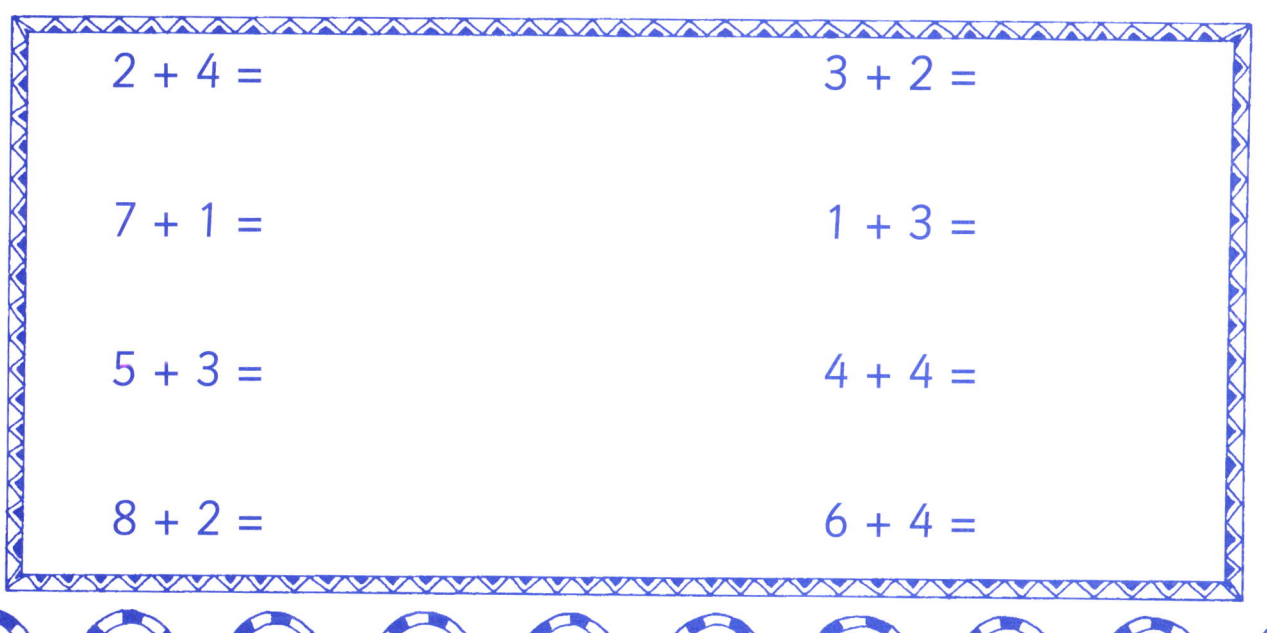

2 + 4 =   3 + 2 =

7 + 1 =   1 + 3 =

5 + 3 =   4 + 4 =

8 + 2 =   6 + 4 =

1 2 3 4 5 6 7 8 9 10

Adding machines

Look at the sign and number on each adding machine.
Put each number through the machine
and write the new number in the box.

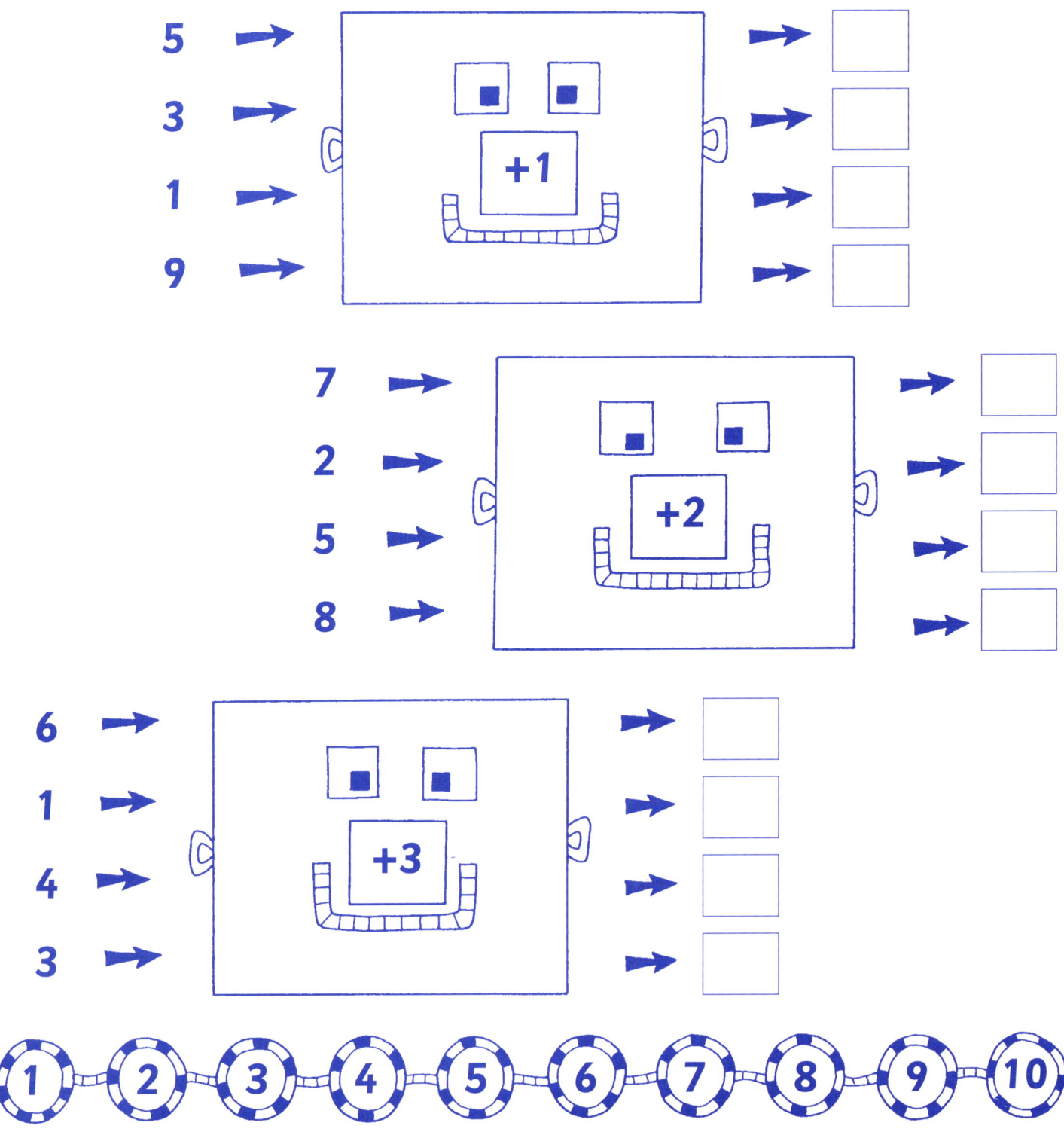

Sorting sets

Each set of objects has its own container. Count the number of objects in each set and draw a line to show where it belongs.

Heavy and light

Look at the pictures. Why is Fred happy
only in the last picture?

What do you think will happen if the elephant
jumps on to the plank?

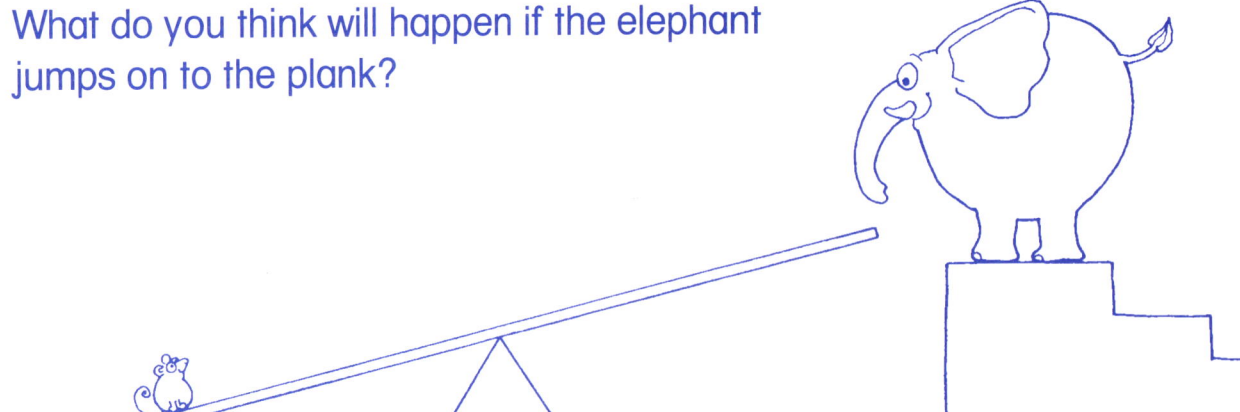

What do you think would happen if the elephant
and the mouse swopped places?

Fred is only happy when he finds a child his size to sit on the other end of the see-saw. Discuss with children how the see-saw works best when it is evenly balanced. Discussing possibilities and predicting outcomes are important mathematical skills.

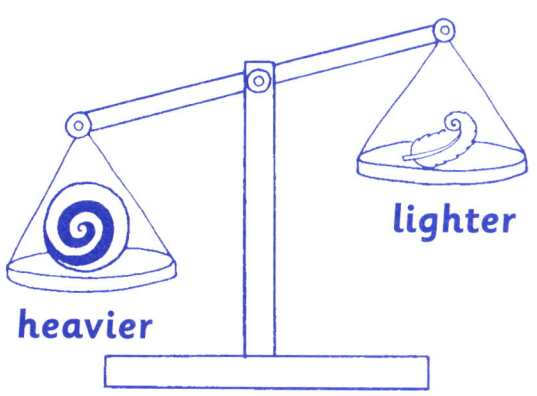

heavier **lighter**

Can you see what happens when you put a feather and a ball on some scales? The feather is lighter than the ball, so the feather moves up and the ball goes down.

Read the question under each set of scales, then answer the question by drawing a tick ✓ in the correct box.

☐ Which is **heavier**? ☐

☐ Which is **lighter**? ☐

☐ Which is **heavier**? ☐

☐ Which is **lighter**? ☐

These exercises show if children understand how scales tip to show which object is heavier. Practical activities using building blocks or beads to balance a toy on scales will give children a very basic understanding of units of measurement.

Take away

Write the answers to these take away sums in the box.

4 lollies.

Take away 1.
Cross it out

How many now?

□

6 sweets.

Take away 2.
Cross them out

How many now?

□

These two sums can also be written like this:

4 − 1 = 3   6 − 2 = 4

− means minus or take away

You need to do a take-away sum to answer each of these sums.
Write the numbers and the answers in the boxes.

You buy 3 buns
and you eat 1.
How many buns
are there now?

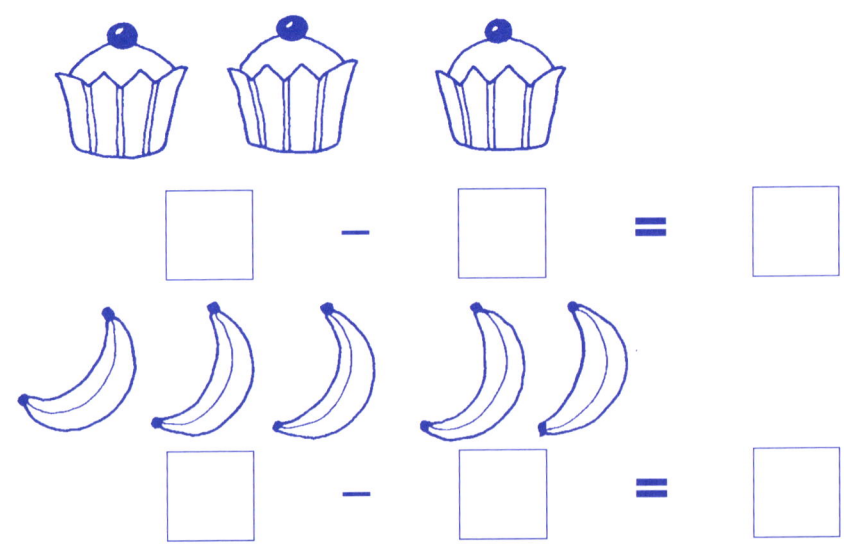

□ − □ = □

You have 5 bananas
and you eat 2.
How many bananas
are there now?

□ − □ = □

Addition, subtraction etc are described in such a variety of ways it is not surprising that
children become confused about what is expected of them. If children are reluctant to write
out sums, focus on the problem solving and ask them how they would show the sum on paper.

You have 4 toy cars, but your sister takes 1 away. How many cars do you have now?

□ – □ = □

You win 6 marbles, then you lose 2. How many are there now?

□ – □ = □

You pick 6 blackberries. You eat 3. How many are there now?

□ – □ = □

Write the answers to these sums after the = sign.
Use the number beads to help you.

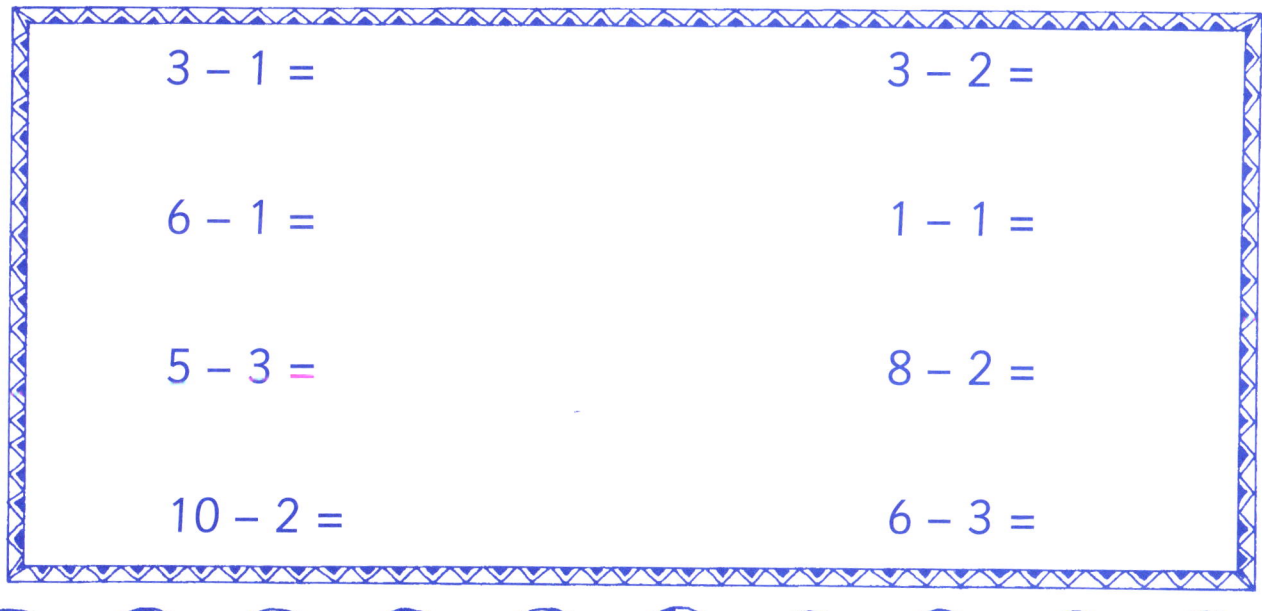

3 – 1 =   3 – 2 =

6 – 1 =   1 – 1 =

5 – 3 =   8 – 2 =

10 – 2 =   6 – 3 =

Take-away machines

Look at the sign and number on each take-away machine.
Put each number through the machine
and write the new number in the box.

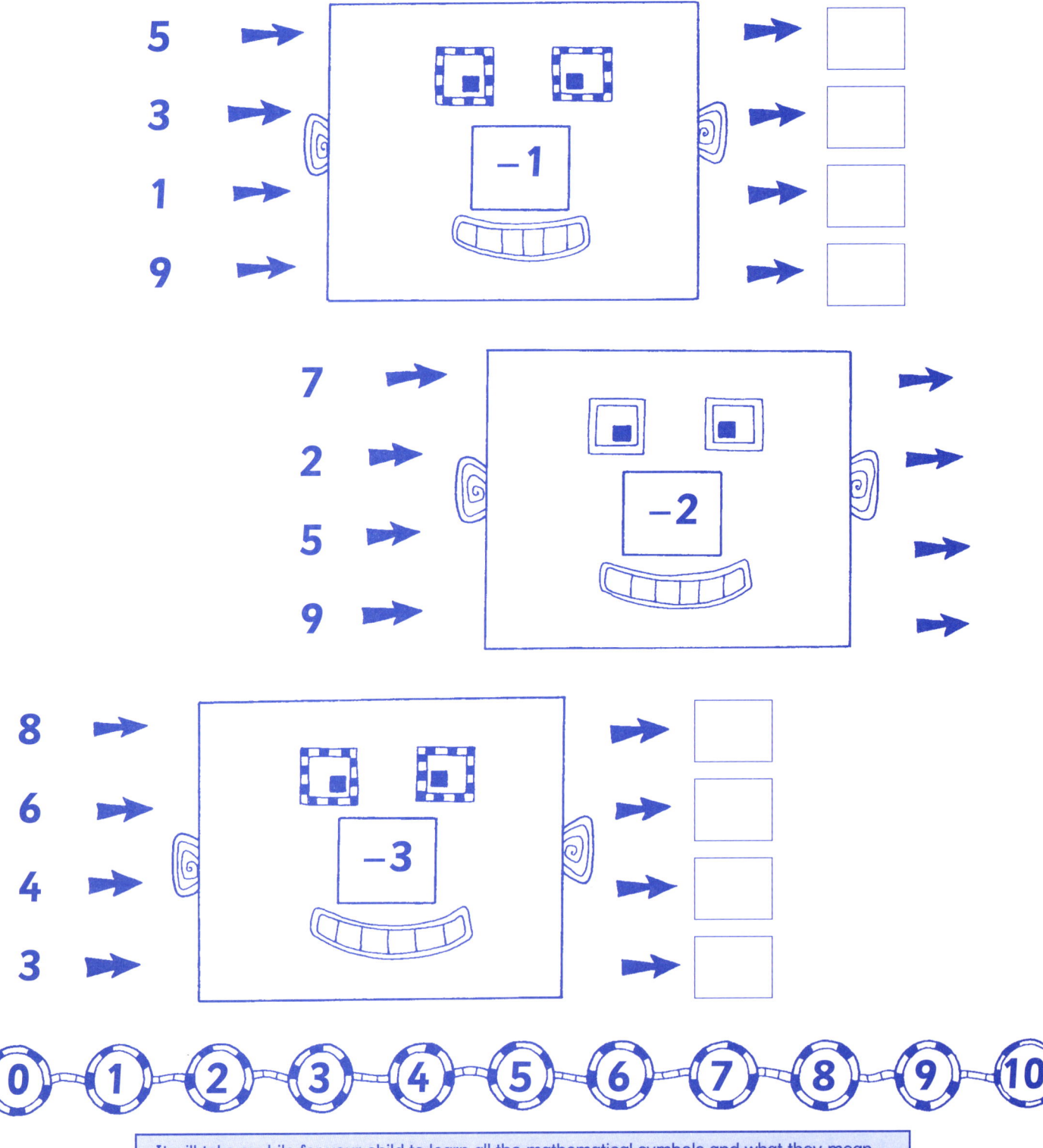

Dot to dot

Join up the dots from 1 to 30 to find out what is chasing Fred.

Tall, small, long and short

Look at the pictures. Why is Sally happy only in the last picture?

Who do you think will reach the boat?

Sally is too small to reach the ball so she needs someone taller to reach it for her. The park keeper has a longer stick so he will reach the boat.

Colour the **longer** snake **red**.

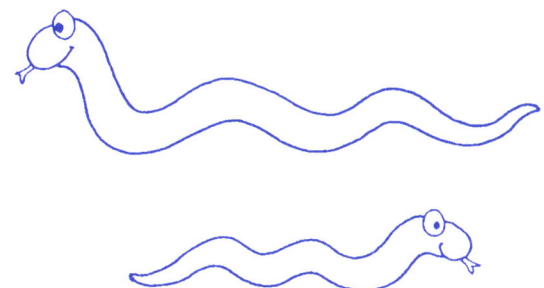

Colour the **shorter** ribbon **blue**.

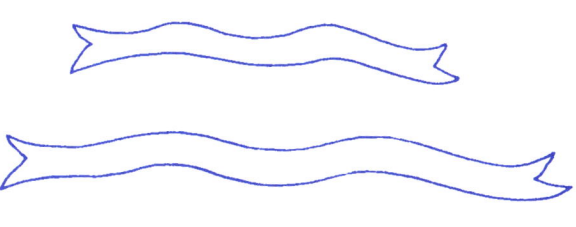

Read the question under each pair of children and answer it by drawing a tick ✓ in the correct box.

☐ Who is smaller? ☐

☐ Who is taller? ☐

Children can only go on this fair ride if they are taller than the measuring stick.

How many children are too small to go on the ride?

Lots of...

Write the answers to these problems in the boxes.

4 rabbits. Each rabbit has 2 ears. How many ears all together?

2 + 2 + 2 + 2 = 8
 This can be written as a sum like this:

4 lots of 2 is 8

4 x 2 = 8

x means **multiply by** or **lots of**

3 stools. Each stool has 3 legs. How many legs all together?

3 + 3 + 3 = 9

3 lots of 3 is 9

This can also be written as a sum like this: **3 x 3 = 9**

A sum is a kind of shorthand. It will take time for children to understand that a problem can be written down in a number of ways and that the aim is usually to use the shortest way.

3 packets. There are 4 cakes in each packet.
How many cakes all together?

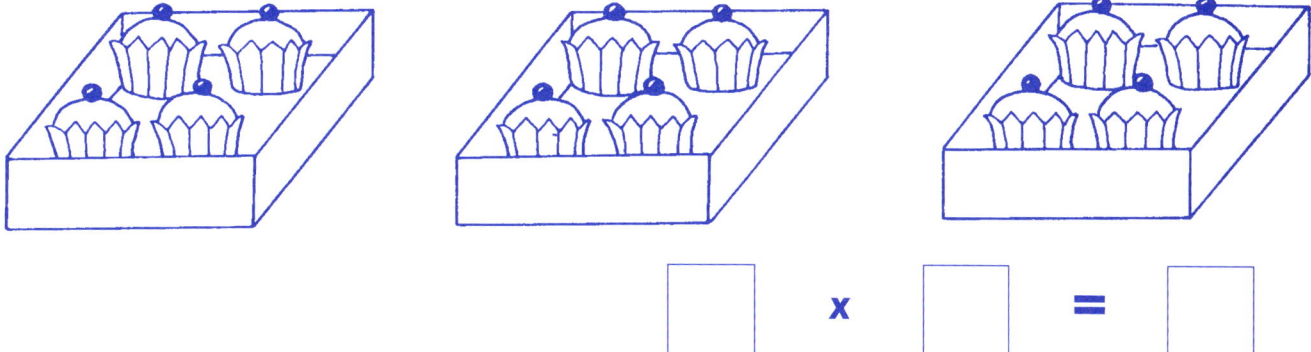

☐ x ☐ = ☐

2 egg boxes. There are six eggs in each box.
How many eggs all together?

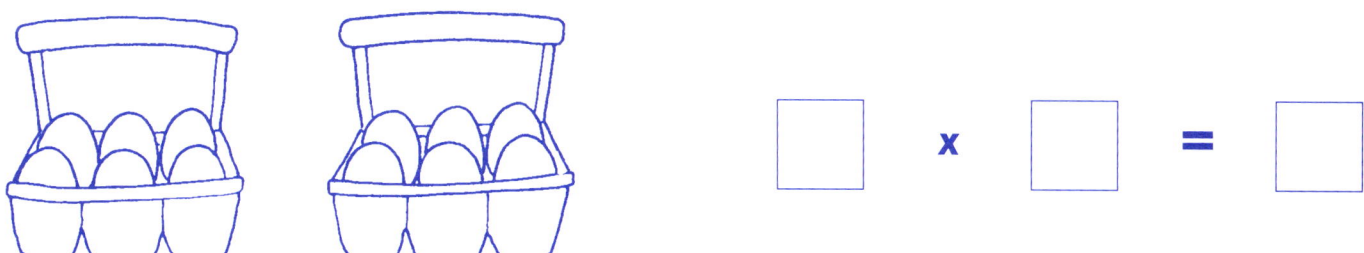

☐ x ☐ = ☐

3 bottles. You can pour 4 glasses of lemonade from each bottle.
Draw 4 glasses beside each bottle.

Now work out how
many glasses of
lemonade all together.

☐ x ☐ = ☐

Practical problems – for example: we want 6 cakes, and there are 4 cakes in a packet, so
how many packets do we need to buy? – are a good way to tackle basic multiplication.

How many all together?

Fill in the missing numbers to complete each sum.

An insect has 6 legs.

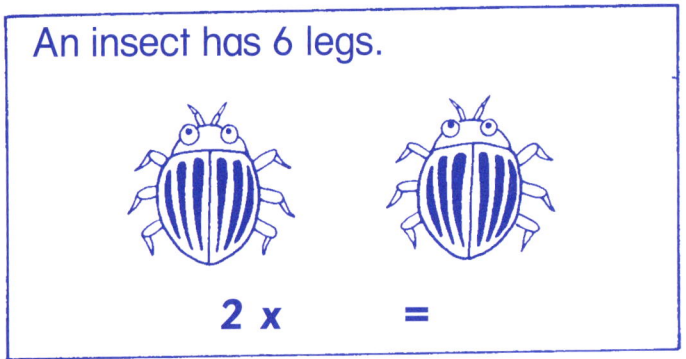

2 x ___ = ___

A chair has 4 legs.

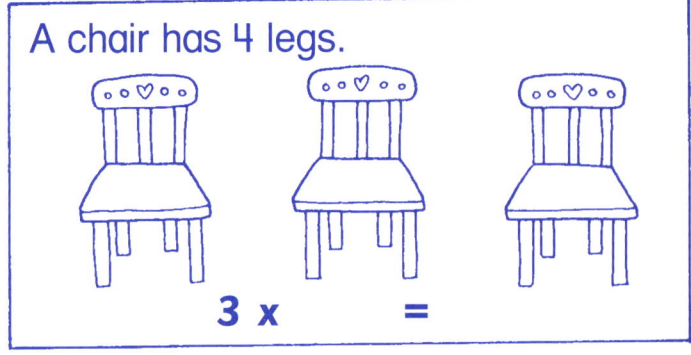

3 x ___ = ___

A star has 5 points.

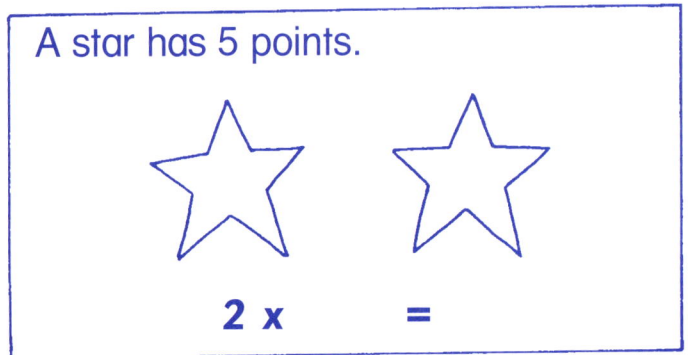

2 x ___ = ___

A triangle has 3 sides.

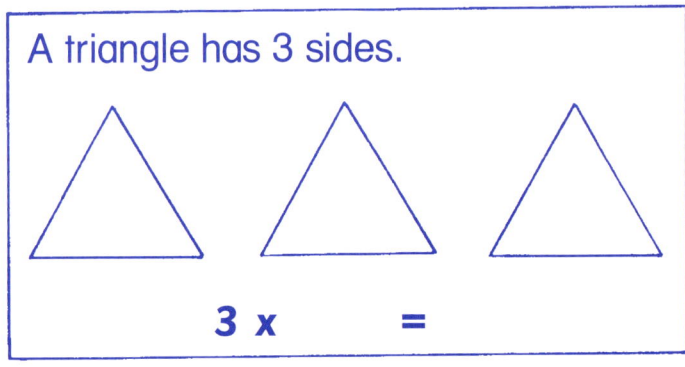

3 x ___ = ___

A goat has 2 horns.

3 x ___ = ___

A spider has 8 legs.

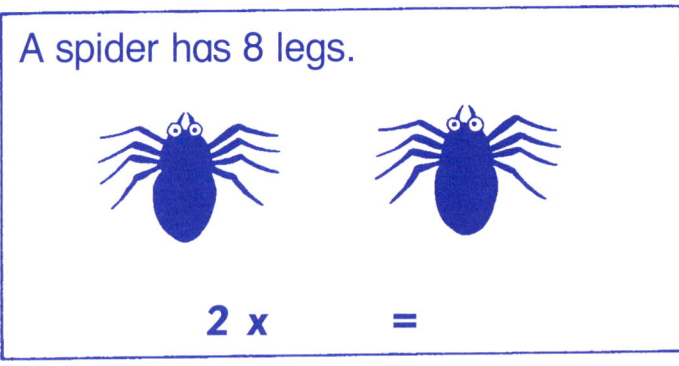

2 x ___ = ___

A week has 7 days.

| Monday | Tuesday | Wednesday | Thursday | Friday | Saturday | Sunday |

| Monday | Tuesday | Wednesday | Thursday | Friday | Saturday | Sunday |

2 x ___ = ___

Toy trips

Lisa has 12 toys
to tidy away.
Lisa can carry
2 toys at a time.

So Lisa makes **6** trips to the toybox.

If Lisa's brother Tom helps they can carry 3 toys.

How many trips to the toy box?

If Lisa uses a cart she can take 6 toys at a time.

How many trips this time?

Dividing

Write the answers to these sums in the boxes.

4 kites and 4 children.   Draw the strings.   How many kites each?

6 balloons and 3 babies.   Draw the strings.   How many balloons each?

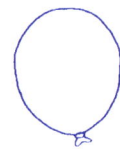  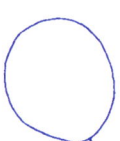 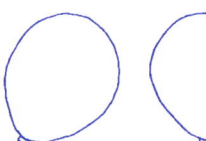   

These two sums can also be written like this:

4 ÷ 4 = 1   **6 ÷ 3 = 2**

÷ means **divided by** or **shared by**

These children want to play football. Draw a line
to show how they can be divided into 2 equal teams.

Write this
as a sum:

| 10 | ÷ | 2 | = | |

Draw lines to show how these children can be
divided into 3 teams.

Write this
as a sum:

| | ÷ | | = | |

The sheep dog needs to divide the sheep into 4
equal groups. Draw a line around each group.

Write this
as a sum:

| | ÷ | | = | |

It takes time and practice for children to understand the uses of division,
but if they understand the concept in a very basic way they can build on that.

Money

Tom, Liz, Bill and Gill have money to spend at the school fair. Guess who has the most money, then count up the coins and write each total in the box. Was your guess correct?

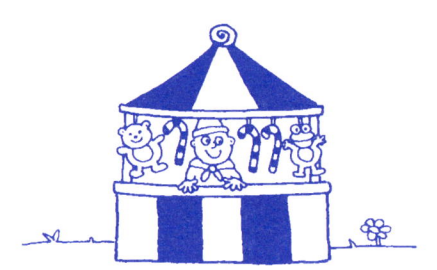

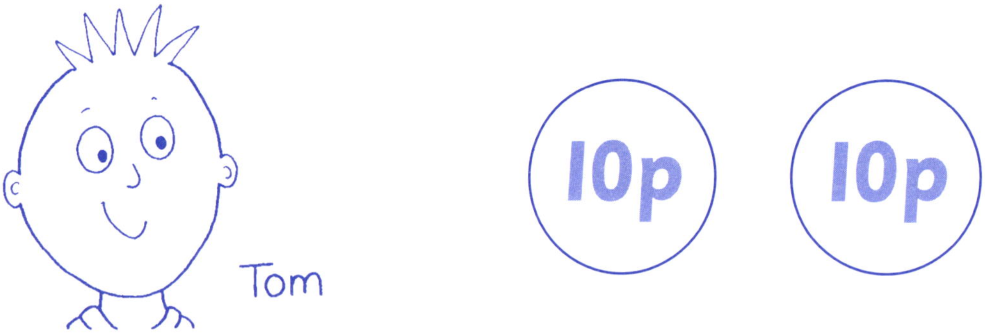
Tom
10p
10p

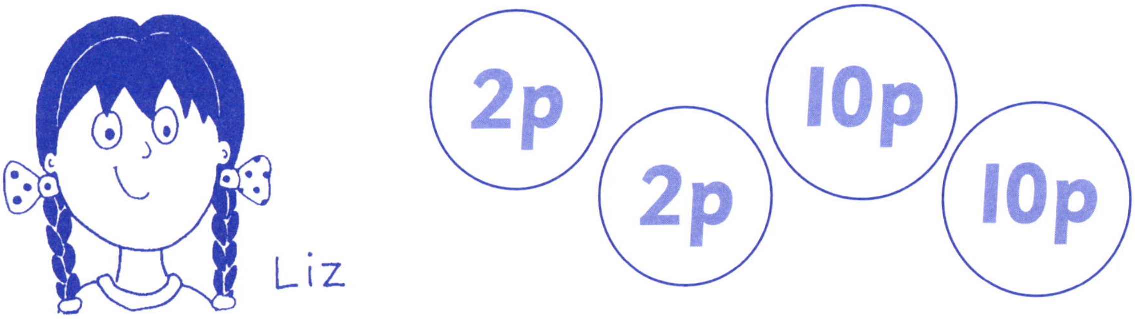
Liz
2p
2p
10p
10p

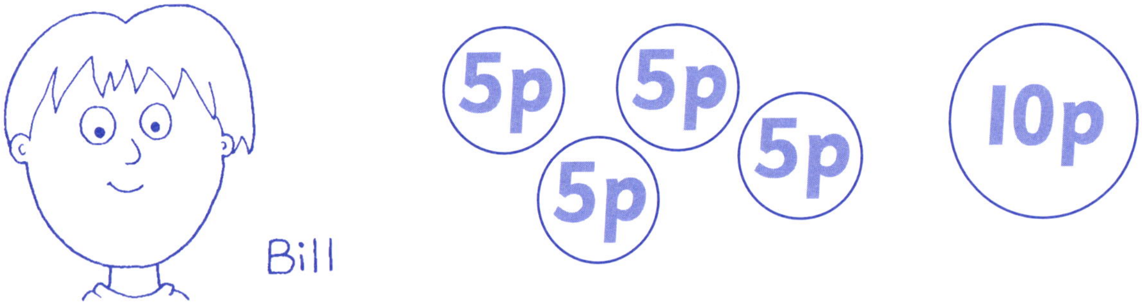
Bill
5p
5p
5p
5p
10p

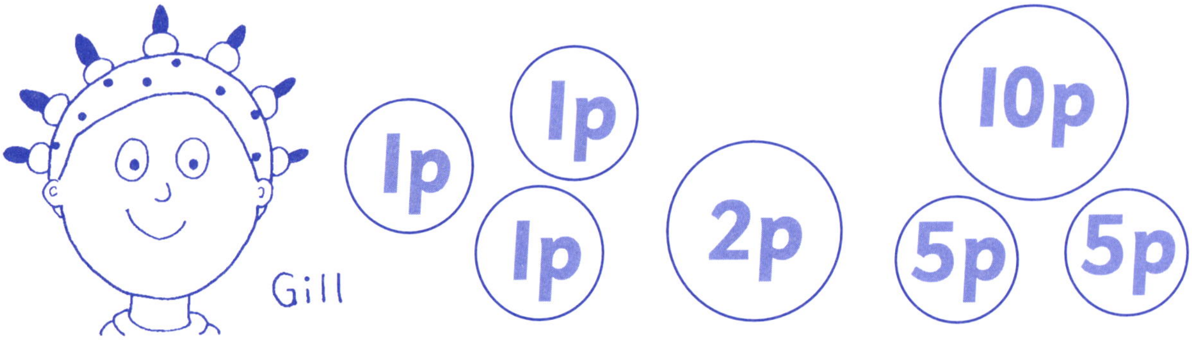
Gill
1p
1p
1p
2p
10p
5p
5p

Children are asked to guess first here to find out if they realise that each coin has a different value. Young children often think that more coins mean more money.

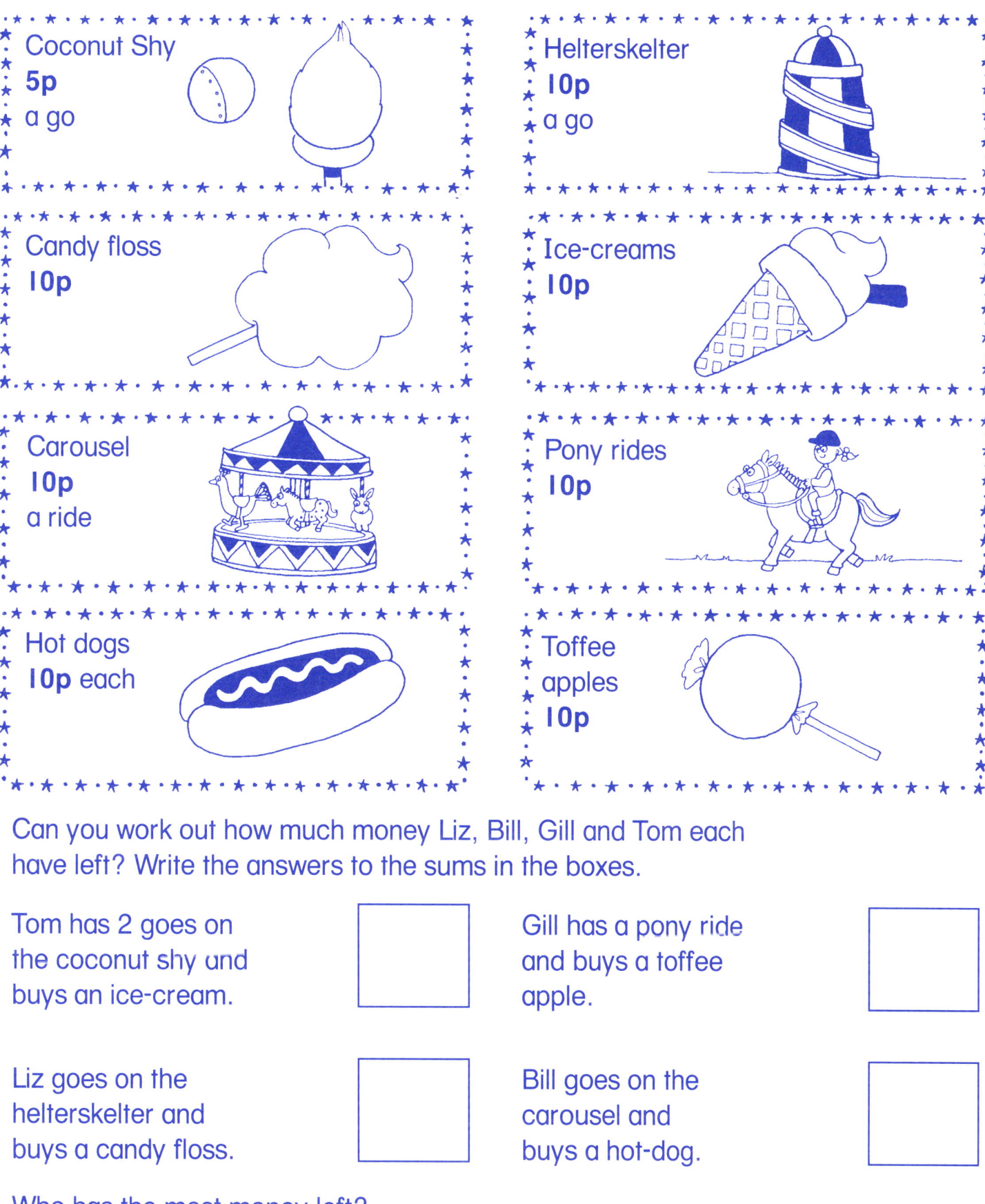

Coconut Shy
5p a go

Helterskelter
10p a go

Candy floss
10p

Ice-creams
10p

Carousel
10p a ride

Pony rides
10p

Hot dogs
10p each

Toffee apples
10p

Can you work out how much money Liz, Bill, Gill and Tom each have left? Write the answers to the sums in the boxes.

Tom has 2 goes on the coconut shy and buys an ice-cream.

Gill has a pony ride and buys a toffee apple.

Liz goes on the helterskelter and buys a candy floss.

Bill goes on the carousel and buys a hot-dog.

Who has the most money left?

Children can work out the sums by crossing out the coins to show how much each child spent. Or your child might like to write down the sums.

Splodged sums!

Oops! Someone has splodged paint all over the page. Can you work out the hidden numbers in these sums?

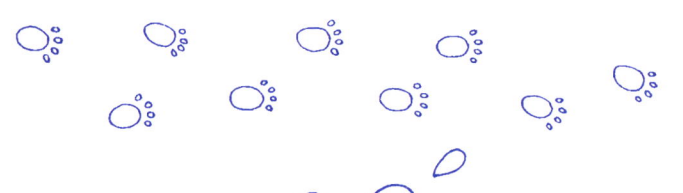

2 + 🟦 = 6

7 + 🟦 = 8

5 + 🟦 = 6

10 − 🟦 = 9

7 − 🟦 = 6

2 x 🟦 = 8

8 ÷ 🟦 = 4

3 + 🟦 = 4

5 + 🟦 = 7

6 − 🟦 = 4

9 − 🟦 = 7

6 − 🟦 = 2

7 x 🟦 = 7

6 ÷ 🟦 = 3